Francis Frith's
AROUND SCARBOROL

PHOTOGRAPHIC MEMORIES

Francis Frith's
AROUND SCARBOROUGH

◆

Dennis Needham

FRITH
BOOK Co

First published in the United Kingdom in 1999 by
Frith Book Company Ltd

British Library Cataloguing in Publication Data

Around Scarborough
Dennis Needham
ISBN 1-85937-104-3

Frith Book Company Ltd
Frith's Barn, Teffont,
Salisbury, Wiltshire SP3 5QP
Tel: +44 (0) 1722 716 376
Email: frithbook.co.uk

Printed and bound in Great Britain

CONTENTS

FRANCIS FRITH: *Victorian Pioneer*

FRANCIS FRITH, Victorian founder of the world-famous photographic archive, was a complex and multitudinous man. A devout Quaker and a highly successful Victorian businessman, he was both philosophic by nature and pioneering in outlook.

By 1855 Francis Frith had already established a wholesale grocery business in Liverpool, and sold it for the astonishing sum of £200,000, which is the equivalent today of over £15,000,000. Now a multi-millionaire, he was able to indulge his passion for travel. As a child he had pored over travel books written by early explorers, and his fancy and imagination had been stirred by family holidays to the sublime mountain regions of Wales and Scotland. 'What a land of spirit-stirring and enriching scenes and places!' he had written. He was to return to these scenes of grandeur in later years to 'recapture the thousands of vivid and tender memories', but with a different purpose. Now in his thirties, and captivated by the new science of photography, Frith set out on a series of pioneering journeys to the Nile regions that occupied him from 1856 until 1860.

INTRIGUE AND ADVENTURE

He took with him on his travels a specially-designed wicker carriage that acted as both dark-room and sleeping chamber. These far-flung journeys were packed with intrigue and adventure. In his life story, written when he was sixty-three, Frith tells of being held captive by bandits, and of fighting 'an awful midnight battle to the very point of surrender with a deadly pack of hungry, wild dogs'. Sporting flowing Arab costume, Frith arrived at Akaba by camel seventy years before Lawrence, where he encountered 'desert princes and rival sheikhs, blazing with jewel-hilted swords'.

During these extraordinary adventures he was assiduously exploring the desert regions bordering the Nile and patiently recording the antiquities and peoples with his camera. He was the first photographer to venture beyond the sixth cataract. Africa was still the mysterious 'Dark Continent', and Stanley and Livingstone's historic meeting was a decade into the future. The conditions for picture taking confound belief. He laboured for hours in his wicker dark-room in the sweltering heat of the desert, while the volatile chemicals fizzed dangerously in their trays. Often he was forced to work in remote tombs and caves where conditions were cooler. Back in London he exhibited his photographs and was 'rapturously cheered' by members of the Royal Society. His reputation as a photographer was made overnight. An eminent modern historian has likened their impact on the population of the time to that on our own generation of the first photographs taken on the surface of the moon.

VENTURE OF A LIFE-TIME

Characteristically, Frith quickly spotted the opportunity to create a new business as a specialist publisher of photographs. He lived in an era of immense and sometimes violent change. For the poor in the early part of Victoria's reign work was a drudge and the hours long, and people had precious little free time to enjoy themselves.

Most had no transport other than a cart or gig at their disposal, and had not travelled far beyond the boundaries of their own town or village. However, by the 1870s, the railways had threaded their way across the country, and Bank Holidays and half-day Saturdays had been made obligatory by Act of Parliament. All of a sudden the ordinary working man and his family were able to enjoy days out and see a little more of the world.

With characteristic business acumen, Francis Frith foresaw that these new tourists would enjoy having souvenirs to commemorate their days out. In 1860 he married Mary Ann Rosling and set out with the intention of photographing every city, town and village in Britain. For the next thirty years he travelled the country by train and by pony and trap, producing fine photographs of seaside resorts and beauty spots that were keenly bought by millions of Victorians. These prints were painstakingly pasted into family albums and pored over during the dark nights of winter, rekindling precious memories of summer excursions.

THE RISE OF FRITH & CO

Frith's studio was soon supplying retail shops all over the country. To meet the demand he gathered about him a small team of photographers, and published the work of independent artist-photographers of the calibre of Roger Fenton and Francis Bedford. In order to gain some understanding of the scale of Frith's business one only has to look at the catalogue issued by Frith & Co in 1886: it runs to some 670

pages, listing not only many thousands of views of the British Isles but also many photographs of most European countries, and China, Japan, the USA and Canada – note the sample page shown above from the hand-written *Frith & Co* ledgers detailing pictures taken. By 1890 Frith had created the greatest specialist photographic publishing company in the world, with over 2,000 outlets – more than the combined number that Boots and WH Smith have today! The picture on the right shows the *Frith & Co* display board at Ingleton in the Yorkshire Dales. Beautifully constructed with mahogany frame and gilt inserts, it could display up to a dozen local scenes.

POSTCARD BONANZA

The ever-popular holiday postcard we know today took many years to develop. In 1870 the Post Office issued the first plain cards, with a pre-printed stamp on one face. In 1894 they allowed other publishers' cards to be sent through the mail with an attached adhesive halfpenny stamp. Demand grew rapidly, and in 1895 a new size of postcard was permitted called the court card, but there was little room for illustration. In 1899, a year after Frith's death, a new card measuring 5.5 x 3.5 inches became the standard format, but it was not until 1902 that the divided back came into being, with address and message on one face and a full-size illustration on the other. *Frith & Co* were in the vanguard of postcard development, and Frith's sons Eustace and Cyril continued their father's monumental task, expanding the number of views offered to the public and recording more and more places in Britain, as the coasts and countryside were opened up to mass travel.

Francis Frith died in 1898 at his villa in Cannes, his great project still growing. The archive he created continued in business for another seventy years. By 1970 it contained over a third of a million pictures of 7,000 cities, towns and villages. The massive photographic record Frith has left to us stands as a living monument to a special and very remarkable man.

Frith's Archive: *A Unique Legacy*

FRANCIS FRITH'S legacy to us today is of immense significance and value, for the magnificent archive of evocative photographs he created provides a unique record of change in 7,000 cities, towns and villages throughout Britain over a century and more. Frith and his fellow studio photographers revisited locations many times down the years to update their views, compiling for us an enthralling and colourful pageant of British life and character.

We tend to think of Frith's sepia views of Britain as nostalgic, for most of us use them to conjure up memories of places in our own lives with which we have family associations. It often makes us forget that to Francis Frith they were records of daily life as it was actually being lived in the cities, towns and villages of his day. The Victorian age was one of great and often bewildering change for ordinary people, and though the pictures evoke an impression of slower times, life was as busy and hectic as it is today.

We are fortunate that Frith was a photographer of the people, dedicated to recording the minutiae of everyday life. For it is this sheer wealth of visual data, the painstaking chronicle of changes in dress, transport, street layouts, buildings, housing, engineering and landscape that captivates us so much today. His remarkable images offer us a powerful link with the past and with the lives of our ancestors.

TODAY'S TECHNOLOGY

Computers have now made it possible for Frith's many thousands of images to be accessed almost instantly. In the Frith archive today, each photograph is carefully 'digitised' then stored on a CD Rom. Frith archivists can locate a single photograph amongst thousands within seconds. Views can be catalogued and sorted under a variety of categories of place and content to the immediate benefit of researchers. Inexpensive reference prints can be created for them at the touch of a mouse button, and a wide range of books and other printed materials assembled and published for a wider, more general readership - in the next twelve months over a hundred Frith local history titles will be published! The

See Frith at www. francisfrith.co.uk

day-to-day workings of the archive are very different from how they were in Francis Frith's time: imagine the herculean task of sorting through eleven tons of glass negatives as Frith had to do to locate a particular sequence of pictures! Yet the archive still prides itself on maintaining the same high standards of excellence laid down by Francis Frith, including the painstaking cataloguing and indexing of every view.

It is curious to reflect on how the internet now allows researchers in America and elsewhere greater instant access to the archive than Frith himself ever enjoyed. Many thousands of individual views can be called up on screen within seconds on one of the Frith internet sites, enabling people living continents away to revisit the streets of their ancestral home town, or view places in Britain where they have enjoyed holidays. Many overseas researchers welcome the chance to view special theme selections, such as transport, sports, costume and ancient monuments.

We are certain that Francis Frith would have heartily approved of these modern developments, for he himself was always working at the very limits of Victorian photographic technology.

THE VALUE OF THE ARCHIVE TODAY

Because of the benefits brought by the computer, Frith's images are increasingly studied by social historians, by researchers into genealogy and ancestry, by architects, town planners, and by teachers and schoolchildren involved in local history projects. In addition, the archive offers every one of us a unique opportunity to examine the places where we and our families have lived and worked down the years. Immensely successful in Frith's own era, the archive is now, a century and more on, entering a new phase of popularity.

THE PAST IN TUNE WITH THE FUTURE

Historians consider the Francis Frith Collection to be of prime national importance. It is the only archive of its kind remaining in private ownership and has been valued at a million pounds. However, this figure is now rapidly increasing as digital technology enables more and more people around the world to enjoy its benefits.

Francis Frith's archive is now housed in an historic timber barn in the beautiful village of Teffont in Wiltshire. Its founder would not recognize the archive office as it is today. In place of the many thousands of dusty boxes containing glass plate negatives and an all-pervading odour of photographic chemicals, there are now ranks of computer screens. He would be amazed to watch his images travelling round the world at unimaginable speeds through network and internet lines.

The archive's future is both bright and exciting. Francis Frith, with his unshakeable belief in making photographs available to the greatest number of people, would undoubtedly approve of what is being done today with his lifetime's work. His photographs, depicting our shared past, are now bringing pleasure and enlightenment to millions around the world a century and more after his death.

SCARBOROUGH – *An Introduction*

SCARBOROUGH IS a town for all seasons, managing to be brash and beautiful, raucous and restrained, ancient and modern, all at the same time.

It is believed to have been established by Norsemen around 966, and sacked by other Norsemen around the time of the Norman Conquest. But before that, Iron Age settlers took over the hill that dominates (and divides) the town. Evidence of their fortified settlement between 700BC and 400BC has been discovered. Two Norse brothers - Kormak and Thorgills - were marauding along the coast when the latter saw Scarborough as a place to settle: he was evidently a man of impeccable taste. He had been born with a harelip and rejoiced in the nickname Scarthi, 'harelip' in Norse. Add in their word for a hill, Burg, and the origins of the town's name becomes clear.

Little is recorded of the fishing village until the Civil War. But we do know that in 1225 Henry III granted 40 royal oaks to be used in the building of a harbour, and that he also granted Scarborough's Charter in 1251. Edward I asked for two warships in 1301 to fight the Scots off Berwick-on-Tweed. The town's castle was twice besieged during the Civil War; on both occasions, the Parliamentarian besiegers starved out the defending Royalists. About this time a certain Mrs Elizabeth Farrow was making claims about the wonderful properties of a small stream which flowed across the beach on what is now Foreshore Road. It was claimed that drinking it would cleanse the stomach and blood, and would be a cure for asthma, jaundice, leprosy, melancholy, scurvy and other ills. For a time, Scarborough had hopes of developing this spring into a spa where the great and the good - to say nothing of the wealthy - would come and be cured. Inland, Harrogate, north of Leeds, was also attempting to tap this early market for tourists.

Owing in no small part to its remoteness, the idea of a spa resort never really achieved the popularity the townspeople hoped for. But the concept of a seaside holiday was taking shape. One Scarborough 'first' that the locals insist is true - although other places make a similar claim - is that the first bathing machines were built and used here. There is a written record of them being hired out by three ladies in 1797. These temples to modesty were taken down to the water whilst their discreet users changed into bathing wear inside. They could then walk down a ramp into the invigorating water showing a minimum of flesh, away from the roving eyes of those who were less than gentlemen. How fashions change; only a generation earlier, bathing in the buff was considered quite the norm.

What did turn the place into a holiday resort was the coming of the railway. The self-styled Railway King - George Hudson - was the first to drive the iron road into the town; this

Scarborough became a magnet for the hordes from the industrialised areas of the West Riding. Guest houses flourished, and a whole range of attractions were developed to keep these new visitors interested. Much of the town is built on a plateau overlooking the two bays. To allow easy access from the town to the beach, three cliff railways were built on the south bay which operate to this day, offering spectacular views on the short ride. A further one - now closed - also used to operate on the north side of the bay.

Towering over Foreshore Road between

was on 7 July 1845, when Scarborough and York were linked. Subsequently, a line south to Filey, Bridlington and Kingston-upon-Hull would be built. An even more scenic route saw trains leave to the north for Whitby, Redcar and Middlesbrough. This was a dramatic route, disconcertingly close to the cliffs at times; it made for a sensational journey. This line closed in 1958, although some of the track bed is still available to walkers.

By the time Victoria was on the throne, cheap travel and some limited time off work had introduced holidays to the lower classes.

two of the cliff railways is Scarborough's most outstanding building. The Grand Hotel is a multi-storeyed building that had a staggering 365 rooms, and was once busy summer and winter. This hotel continued to thrive until modern economics eventually caught up with it. But if opulence and fashion are no more, it is still a popular hotel; it is run by the Butlin group, and continues to offer comfort and the finest of views. But somehow a late night karaoke session does not quite fit the image it used to have. The building was opened in 1867 on a site previously occupied by number

2 The Cliffe, where Ann Bronte died. She used Scarborough as the background to her novel 'Agnes Grey'; she and her sister Charlotte loved the town.   Stricken with tuberculosis, for her last journey she struggled painfully from Haworth in the West over the defences in a most spectacular fashion. Yet the construction of this coastal drive caused uproar in the town. It was well over a century ago that the first plan for Foreshore Road, Marine Drive and Royal Albert Road was mooted. The environment lobby did not

Riding to her beloved Scarborough, and died there on 28 May 1849.

The rest of the area - known as St Nicholas Cliff - is another fine area to explore, with its fine buildings and an iron bridge spanning Valley Road. Close by is The Crescent, an oval road with a tree-covered central green. Around stand superb and most elegant brown sandstone Regency-style houses. Further back from the sea there is a thriving commercial centre with all the major shopping chains in business alongside the local ones. Again, many of the buildings are superb examples of Victorian and Edwardian architecture.

The promontory on which the castle is built effectively divides the coastal strip into the South Bay and the North Bay. Linking this is the Marine Drive, an area that suffers ferocious storms from time to time; the road is often closed, with the violent sea cascading

hold the sway then that they do today, and the work was instituted. The last section to be completed was the Marine Drive, finally opened in 1908. A small toll house close to the east pier is a reminder that road tolls were payable even then.

The south beach area is the most commercialised. Fast food, candy floss and tacky gifts abound. But to compensate for this, the harbour is always interesting, with the remains of a fishing fleet discharging their cargo alongside the west pier. With the few local small fishing craft known as cobles, larger vessels still visit to land their catch and see it auctioned in the shed. But this is a pale shadow of former days when herring were still plentiful. Scarborough would be a calling point for the hundreds of drifters that followed the 'silver darlings' on their migration south. Look for the stalls selling delicious locally caught shellfish alongside the hot dog stands. A freshly-cooked dressed crab has few equals when it comes to taste and flavour.

The lifeboat station is located close by. Across the road was the site of the original lifeboat station. As traffic on the road increased, it was decided to re-locate somewhere more convenient. The old station was sold in the early 1960s to Jaconelli's, a local ice cream maker. They paid £11,000 for it, tore down the old building, and replaced it with something more appropriate to their trade. The story is still told of how old Mrs Jaconelli, signing a cheque for a - then - substantial sum, could not understand how an old shed could be worth so much.

The oldest part of the harbour is still almost exclusively the preserve of working boats. It is sad that the days of assorted cargo boats discharging on the quay along Sandside are no more. Scandinavian timber boats were once regular visitors, but the small port was unable to handle the size of vessel increasingly in use today. Yachts and cruisers can be found in the newer section to the east. East Pier is the amusement pier. There is a huge funfair with exciting rides. On the Lighthouse Pier, there are the two boats that offer pleasure trips out into the bay and for several miles north to Ravenscar or south to Filey Brig. There are some ancient buildings close to the harbour. Quay Street has one that dates to 1300. Opposite the old harbour in Sandside is Richard III's House. The king is reputed to have stayed here in 1483, although the medieval building was refaced in Elizabethan times.

Entertainment in Scarborough is available in profusion. The Futurist Theatre offers live shows throughout the season and also some in winter; the locals like to be entertained as well. You can also see the occasional cinema show here. The Spa complex was always the draw for older visitors. Here, you could relax, sit in a deck chair and listen to the Palm Court Orchestra playing beautiful melodies all afternoon. The Spa Orchestra still entertain during the summer, but other variety shows tend now to dominate the evenings. In winter, the place is used as a conference cen-

tre, which draws much needed trade for off-season hotels and restaurants.

But Scarborough is also at the very leading edge of theatrical entertainment. In the town centre, opposite the train station, a former cinema has recently opened as Scarborough's Theatre-in-the-Round. Here, the famous English playwright Alan Ayckbourn premieres his new productions. Alan is a long-time resident of the town. His concept of theatre is to do away with a stage and proscenium arch, and to seat the audience around a central area where the action takes place. Very intimate it is too. Another thespian connection with the town is that it was the birthplace of Charles Laughton, whose parents were hoteliers. Born in 1899, his first theatrical performance as an amateur in 1923 was in 'Hobson's Choice'. His rise was meteoric: by 1932 he had won an Oscar for his role at Henry VIII in the film 'The Private Life of Henry VIII'.

Although Scarborough is not the genteel, slightly up-market place it once was, there are still enough superb buildings, wonderful views and fine shops to keep it high on the list of places that are well worth a visit.

South Beach

If EVER there was an area that could be accused of being schizoid, this is it. On the one hand, there is a fascinating harbour, ancient buildings, narrow alleys to explore and miles of golden sand. Then, there is another side: crowds of holidaymakers, fish and chip shops beyond count and loads of amusement arcades. Exactly how you take the South Beach depends to a great extent on when you visit. If peaceful appreciation of the town's history is your preference, any time off-season is fine. But even then, on a sunny winter's day there will be plenty of people about. A brisk stroll along Foreshore Road soon after breakfast, even in the height of the season, can be an invigorating and pleasant experience.

The beach itself extends past the Spa before turning rocky. There is a bathing pool - opened in 1915 - together with extensive formal gardens. Indeed, one delightful walk is to take the cliff railway at Valley Road and turn left over the iron bridge spanning the valley. Beyond the Spa is a beautiful rose garden followed by a striking Italian garden.

The paths continue southwards towards the Holbeck Gardens and the crumbling Cliffs. This area made the news headlines in June 1993 when the clifftop Holbeck Hotel, with the most exquisite views out to sea, literally fell down the cliff as erosion caused its foundations to give way.

In earlier days, the Spa was very much an ad hoc arrangement where visitors drank the highly-coloured - and strange-tasting - water, secure in the knowledge that it would improve their general health. It took the Victorians to develop the area properly. The magnificent Spa buildings were originally built in the 1850s to a design by Sir Joseph Paxton. Unfortunately, these did not survive a fire in 1876, and the whole area was rebuilt. This complex lasted for almost a century; then extensive refurbishment took place, which managed to retain the essentially Victorian opulence of the building whilst providing the sort of facilities expected today.

A fine example of this opulence was seen when the first Earl Londesborough, who was immensely rich and had a villa in The Crescent, invited his friend the Prince of Wales to make three royal visits to Scarborough between 1869 and 1871: a mile of red carpet was laid out to allow the Prince to walk from The Crescent to the Spa.

The cliff railway here avoids the necessity of taking 224 steps up to the Esplanade. This was the first of its kind to be built in England and opened in 1875. It is operated by a counter-balanced cable-hauled hydraulic system, and provides access to some of Scarborough's finest hotels and guest houses. One of the finest - The Crown Hotel - was opened in 1844 and advertised extensively. This brought a clientele from all over the world, as it still does.

SOUTH BAY C1873 6560
Looking north from the end of the Esplanade.
Note the many bathing machines still in use, and
the recently completed Grand Hotel on the left.
The area at the foot of the cliffs will eventually
become Foreshore Road.

SOUTH BAY c1885 18233
The buildings in the foreground are part of the recently completed Spa complex. The tide is clearly well out, and bathing machines are still in evidence.

SOUTH BAY c1885 18235
A view from the Belmont Road area, revealing in more detail the sheer magnificence of the Grand Hotel. The four cupolas are clearly visible.

THE BEACH C1885 18237
A sizeable crowd gathers to watch a Punch and Judy show. These one-man shows, which reached the height of their popularity in Victorian times, were based on the character of Pulcinella, the impudent hunchback from the Commedia dell'Arte, which originated in 16th-century Italy.

SOUTH BAY 1886 18240

Victorian modesty is evident, with ankle-length dresses being worn at the height of summer. One Victorian dress would provide enough material for a dozen or more outfits today, when bikinis rule the beach. Note the building to the extreme left: this is the foot of the newly introduced Cliff Railway.

SOUTH CLIFF TRAMWAY 1890 23459

Here we see the Cliff Railway in its entirety. Opened only five years before this picture was taken, the fare was 1d, the old penny being worth about .4 of a post-decimalisation one. It offered visitors who stayed in the elegant buildings at the top - along the Esplanade - the chance of reaching the Spa without having to negotiate 224 steps.

SANDS AND GRAND HOTEL 1890
Bathing machines can be seen in abundance in this view. Much of the building work along Foreshore Road that created the holiday resort is now completed. The Grand Hotel is to left of centre.

SPA AND SANDS 1890
Another crowded scene on the South Beach close to the Spa, whose ornateness and splendour is clear to see. The Victorian beach was a place to promenade rather than to sit.

SANDS AND GRAND HOTEL 1890 23455

SPA AND SANDS 1890 23453

SPA SALOON 1890 23450
The Spa complex in more detail, showing it after the rebuilding following the disastrous 1876 fire. Note the huge expanse of beach with few people using it. Perhaps they were all around the Spa listening to the small orchestra that would be playing. This scene has changed little over the ensuing century, although crinolines, bowler hats and parasols now tend to be in short supply.

SPA PROMENADE 1890 23452

Another view of the Spa buildings, this time from Promenade level. There is no record of why the huge banners proclaiming Queen Victoria are displayed.

FORESHORE ROAD 1891 28812

From the bottom of Valley Road the camera captures a crowded South Beach scene, and a bay full of sail-driven fishing boats. After the crowded towns of the West Riding, escaping to the broad expanses of beaches like this must have been sheer heaven to the Victorians.

VIEW FROM THE ESPLANADE 1890 23457

This photograph was taken from the Esplanade looking north. The iron footbridge spanning Valley Road can be clearly picked out to the left of and below the Grand Hotel. Night-time illumination comes from the ornate lamp standard that was to become a ubiquitous piece of Victorian street furniture.

GRAND HOTEL AND FORESHORE ROAD 1891 28808

A further view from the path leading to The Esplanade. Bathing machines are still popular.

SANDS AND HARBOUR 1890 23461

The sheer volume of boats in the South Bay is amazing. Most of them appear to be cobles, a traditional Yorkshire open boat easily identified by the square transom which has a reverse slope. Only a small number remain today, now relying on the internal combustion engine for power, rather than the wind.

SANDS AND GRAND HOTEL 1890

Pictured from the beach, the sheer extent of the Grand Hotel becomes plain. A chance to sample its opulence would be high on the wish list of many visitors, passing en route to their boarding houses after a happy day on the beach.

SOUTH BAY 1891

Here we see South Bay with a plentiful array of bathing machines. These allowed the ladies a chance to change into their swimwear and step into the sea some distance from the lustful eyes of any male.

SANDS AND GRAND HOTEL 1890 23456

SOUTH BAY 1891 28809

SOUTH CLIFF 1897 39453

A busy scene on the Esplanade above The Spa. The motive power of the day - horses - marked their passage quite clearly, and ladies didn't just dirty their shoes; ankle length dresses would easily become soiled. The sheer number of people forces them to use the road rather than the pavement. The hat is de rigeur to both sexes.

FORESHORE ROAD 1890 23464
Here we see Foreshore Road and South Bay looking south
from the west pier wall. The building on the right with
open doors is the old lifeboat station. Today it is located
across the road on the seaward side, where the slipway is.

SOUTH BAY 1897 39329
With a spring tide, most of the fishing cobles have put to sea, and the amount of available beach is minimal.

SOUTH BAY 1901 46775
Scarborough's expanse of golden sands are well concealed by a particularly high tide. The buildings on the sea shore indicate that the transformation from fishing village to seaside resort is now complete.

'EVENING' 1890 23462
There is plenty of activity in the South Bay as fishing boats are prepared for sea. Taken from the end of the west pier, the picture graphically illustrates the dominance of the Grand Hotel on this part of Scarborough.

FROM THE FISH PIER 1890 23465
Fishing and general cargo boats are at rest in the
South Bay. Despite the railways being well
established , places like Scarborough still relied to
a great extent on goods and supplies being
delivered by sea.

SPA AND SOUTH CLIFF 1891 28811
At sea level on the left is the Spa complex of buildings. Above is the collection of elegant buildings that line the Esplanade and adjoining streets.

BAY FROM HARBOUR 1897 39458
Although the time of year is not recorded, there appears to be a distinct lack of visitors. Foliage on the trees would seem to indicate summer, so perhaps it is an early morning view. As is always the case, there is plenty of activity on and around the boats.

SOUTH BAY, FROM HARBOUR 1897 39459
A fishing coble is being punted away from the beach, apparently loaded with lobster pots. Shellfish were - and are - an important local catch. The elegant footbridge over Valley Road can be seen to the left.

THE BEACH c1955 S71145
The skyline has changed little from the earlier photographs, but
the deck chair is now ubiquitous. Gentlemen's clothing is still
dominated by the suit, but ladies' hem-lines have risen somewhat.
Hats have virtually disappeared.

THE BEACH c1955 S71146

With barely enough room to build a sand castle, the children seem somewhat constrained. The degree of clothing being worn would indicate that the chill easterly breeze that often affects this coast is blowing. Note the name 'Corrigan' on the building in the centre: this family have operated side-shows and amusements in this area for decades, and are active to this day.

THE BEACH c1955 S71148

The dominant building is the new lifeboat station. Launching from here is a relatively simple matter. When it was across the road, horses had to drag the boat out to meet the tide.

THE BEACH C1955 S71150
Two young ladies return from a paddle as a drifter dries its sail before returning to sea in the continued search for the vast shoals of herring that used to migrate southwards in the North Sea. Catching, preparing and smoking the herring was once a major east coast industry. Over-fishing has reduced their numbers to virtually nil.

SANDS AND HARBOUR C1955 S71137
The castle, overlooking the bay, is dominant. A pleasure boat is tied up alongside the Lighthouse Pier, and the helter-skelter of the funfair on east pier can just be picked out.

THE HARBOUR

THE HARBOUR area was once the commercial and industrial heart of Scarborough. Shipbuilding was carried on as well. One of the last companies to close was called Tindalls. An employee of theirs at the time of closure was Edward Harland. In 1858, he moved to Belfast, and continued shipbuilding there. Two years later, he teamed up with Gustav William Wolff, thus creating that famous company which was responsible for the construction of so many fine Atlantic liners and warships. Harland died in 1913.

This area is a magnet to most people visiting the town. Although the EC-regulated fishing fleet is but a pale shadow of its former glory, there is plenty to see - especially at high tide when the boats return. As the water ebbs, the remaining craft will settle on the bottom, and at spring tides, the water will leave the harbour completely.

The old fish auction sheds are still there and in use. It is possible to catch some of the action, usually in the early mornings. Later in the day, mending the nets, that most traditional of pastimes in fishing villages, is practised by the locals. The small coble - a East Coast-style boat not seen outside this area - is still in evidence. The cobles take out crab and lobster pots to the many rocky areas on either side of town to catch these delicacies. At the start of the West Pier are a collection of shellfish stalls. Mainly operated by local fishermen, they sell a whole range of delicious fish. The local tiny winkle vies for shelf space with the mighty oyster, with mussel, whelk and cockle in between. The lifeboat sits in its new shed alongside the harbour walls. The station was established across the road in 1801 and has been responsible for saving almost 900 lives.

The Lighthouse Pier - or Vincent's as it is also known - has (unsurprisingly) the lighthouse on it. Here, also, is the old trawler Hatherleigh. Formerly a deep sea fishing boat, she was retired to Scarborough, where visitors can now climb all over her and try to imagine what it was like fighting mountainous seas in sub-zero temperatures. This pier is also where the pleasure boats arrive and depart. Two of them, MV 'Regal Lady' and MV 'Coronia', have a fascinating history. Both were constructed before the last war, and both answered the call to evacuate the British

Expeditionary Force from the beaches of Dunkirk in 1940. Indeed, 'Coronia', as HMS 'Watchful', is credited with saving over 400 lives.

The two boats have carried millions of happy passengers since then, maintaining a fine tradition of pleasure-cruising on this coast that goes back to the paddle-steamers in the last century.

The East Pier is the newest pier, forming a new harbour that is now the domain of motor launches and yachts. Much of the pier is taken up by an extensive funfair with a wide assortment of slides and side-shows.

REPAIRING LOBSTER POTS c1955 S71132
A timeless picture of fishermen repairing the ravages of sea and lobsters. The fashions of the 1950s are clearly in evidence from the interested watchers.

PIERHEAD 1890 23472

A simply amazing collection of masts, spars, sails and herring drifters in the harbour. The registration letters of the two front boats indicate a home port of Great Yarmouth (YH) and Lowestoft (LT). Having discharged their catch, they would sail out into the North Sea to rejoin the fray. The paddle steamer was one of the early forms of pleasure boat transport that operated from Scarborough.

PIERHEAD 1890 23471

A trip around the bay has been an attraction at Scarborough for many years. Here, a paddle steamer loads another horde of pleasure seekers. To the right of the lighthouse, the smoke stack of another steamer can be seen.

HARBOUR ENTRANCE c1955
A sea cruise remains popular with holidaymakers. The MV 'Coronia' - famed for its part in the 'Little Ships' rescue of the British Expeditionary Force from Dunkirk in 1940 returns to port.

THE HARBOUR c1955
A pleasure cruiser - probably MV 'Regal Lady' - lies moored out of use on the muddy bottom of the new (east) Castle Dock.

HARBOUR ENTRANCE c1955 S71120

THE HARBOUR c1955 S71005

THE LIGHTHOUSE 1890 23470
A sail-powered fishing boat returns to port, ready to unload its catch. Note the smoke stack of a paddle steamer tied to the Lighthouse Pier.

PIERHEAD 1890 23466
A Lowestoft-registered fishing boat leaves harbour
as holidaymakers try their luck fishing in the bay.
The stern of one of the steam-powered pleasure
paddle boats is visible to the right.

CASTLE HILL 1890 23469

Here we see Castle Dock, with an assortment of spars and rigging dominating the view. Today, this area is the preserve of yachts and motor cruisers, who use the water for leisure rather than earning a living.

FISHING BOATS 1890 23467

A row of drifters settled on the South Beach. The sheer volume of boats of all shapes and sizes is staggering. Again, the east coast herring fishing boats are prominent. This view was taken from the west pier.

THE HARBOUR C1955 S71102
A more recent picture of the main harbour. Smaller fishing boats, now powered by internal combustion rather than wind, are tied up alongside the west pier to discharge their catch. The fleet is but a pale shadow of itself compared to previous years.

HARBOUR ENTRANCE c1955 S71126
A peaceful scene as a fishing coble returns to port. The packed harbour of yesteryear is now but a memory, and pleasure boating has not yet really taken off.

THE HARBOUR c1955 S71134
The quay to the left, with Sandside beyond it, is where cargo boats used to discharge into waiting lorries. Timber was a regular trade here. Now, commerce is a rare event. A few rowing boats and one trawler are all that can be seen.

VIEW FROM THE LIGHTHOUSE c1955 S71128
An unusual view, taken from the top of the lighthouse. It clearly shows both harbours with minimal boating activity, but the helter-skelter on the east pier is in place by this time. The castle wall is also clearly visible.

FISHING BOATS IN HARBOUR c1955 S71133
This view of the harbour is taken from the slipway at Sandside. There is no evidence of working boats, but the funfair can be seen. Scarborough is by now almost entirely devoted to entertaining holidaymakers.

CASTLE DOCKS 1890 23468
Castle Dock offers an altogether busier scene with two paddle steamers tied up; the left hand one is ready to go, with a wisp of steam from its siren almost at the top of the smoke stack. An elegant smaller steam launch is on the move almost alongside.

THE HARBOUR ENTRANCE AND TOWN c1955 S71125
St. Mary's church can be seen clearly on the skyline, and an early motor coach of the type that causes so much congestion in Scarborough today can be seen along Sandside.

ROWING BOAT ENTERING HARBOUR c1955 S71121
A lone oarsman makes his way from Sandside towards the west pier, as one of the pleasure boats returns to discharge its cargo of happy holidaymakers. At this time, fishing was still a profitable business. Today, the boatmen earn more ferrying visitors around or into the bay for a day's fishing.

CASTLE FROM THE EAST PIER c1955 S71123

Lighthouse Pier makes a pleasant stroll for all the family. For many years, it was impossible to move here without a photographer snapping you, pushing a card in your hand and telling you to call at his kiosk on the front for some happy holiday snaps.

THE FISH MARKET c1955 S71131

Close to the west pier, these stalls are - and still are - a magnet for shellfish lovers. Fresh dressed crab and lobsters are always on sale, together with all varieties of shellfish. You can buy locally smoked kippers, or send them home or to friends by post. The building at the far end is the lifeboat house.

The Castle

THE CURRENT fortification on this site can be traced back to around 1160. This was during the reign of Henry II, first of the Plantagenet kings. But long before this, the rocky promontory 300ft (91m) above the sea on which the Castle is built was the scene of fortification and settlement. The earliest evidence indicates that Iron and Bronze Age man lived here. The Romans found it, and used it for a signal post; the remains of this are still visible within the walls of the Castle. Later, the Norsemen came calling (and pillaging). During the time that the Castle was in use, several sieges were laid over the centuries. Royal visitors were quite frequent, as it was first choice for the Court when on tour.

The condition of today's ruins is largely due to the efforts of Oliver Cromwell's Roundheads during the Civil War. At the start of the war, Scarborough declared for the King; this was unusual, in that most of the eastern part of England favoured the Roundheads. The Castle was besieged from February to July 1645. Starvation, rather than the constant pounding of cannon located in nearby Peasholm, caused the Castle to surrender. As a result of this siege, the west wall - some 15ft (4.6m) thick - was demolished, although the highest point is still 85ft (26m) tall.

It was then safely in Parliamentarian hands until 1648, when the governor defected to the Royalists. Thus the stage was set for another siege. By coincidence, this also lasted for four months, and again starvation caused the surrender. The Castle itself never fell to pure force of arms, despite several sieges over the centuries. Cromwell ordered the Castle to be partly destroyed so that it could not be used as a fortification again. But as a result of the Jacobite rebellion of 1745, a barracks was built to house the local garrison.

The last forcible adjustment of the Castle occurred as recently as 1914. Two German cruisers took up station off Scarborough, and fired over 500 shells into the defenceless town. Much damage was done to the curtain wall of the Castle, and the 1745 barracks were demolished. This action soon spawned a slogan for the enlistment posters that urged young men to join up and fight the Germans. It ran: 'Remember Scarborough? Enlist Now!'

Probably the Castle's most famous prisoner was George Fox. He was the founder of the Society of Friends (The Quakers), and was incarcerated for a time in 1666.

Today, the keep, barbican and curtain wall still stand. The site covers some 7.69 hectares (19 acres), offering spectacular sea views from the buttressed walls. The property is looked after and maintained by English Heritage; it is open for visitors every day during the summer, and is closed on Monday and Tuesday during the winter.

THE CASTLE 1890 23475
This view is taken from the walls and looks
generally north-west towards the keep. When this
photograph was taken, conservation as we know it
today only interested a few people, who were often
regarded as eccentrics.

THE CASTLE AND WALLS c1955 S71093
Now, with English Heritage in charge, the remains are carefully conserved, and constant attrition from the wind and sea repaired. There is no evidence of the German bombardment in 1914 to see.

THE CASTLE c1955 S71107

This view is taken from outside the walls, looking north. The Sealed Knot stage re-enactments of the 1648 assault on Scarborough Castle with musket, pike and cannon.

NORTH BAY 1891 28822

From the Castle battlements, there was an excellent view to the north. The Pier, destroyed in a gale in 1905, is clearly visible. Visitors are now given an audio tape, player and headphones in the Castle. A vivid description of the place and its history are contained for this guide-yourself-tour.

North Bay

IF THE South Bay is the commercialised, brash face of Scarborough, the North Bay is more refined, perhaps even a little more discreet. Extensive strolls through the glorious colours of Clarence and Alexander Gardens help to create this ambience, and the delightful Queens Parade provides a fine backdrop of Regency buildings.

The Victorians attempted to develop the holiday trade by constructing a chain pier in the bay. Finished in 1869, it cost £16,000 to build, but the location was quite suspect. The way that the sea beats the Marine Drive area should have provided the builders with a warning. Sure enough, one stormy night - 8 January 1905 - the waves battered the elegant ironwork into submission and the North Pier was no more.

Much of Scarborough's green open space is to be found at this end of town. Astonishingly for such a built up area, there are almost 400 acres (160 hectares) of parkland within the town. There is a corner of intense holiday activity at the end of Royal Albert Drive, with water features providing endless fun for the youngsters. A little inland is Peasholm Park. This is pure parkland, just the sort of place to

enjoy a relaxing hour amongst the wonderful floral displays. The latest creation is a Japanese garden, complete with pagoda, waterfall and lanterns. There is boating to keep the youngsters happy, and plenty of other diversions in the immediate area.

The Scarborough Cricket Festival used to be held in September. Recently, July has become the time for this feast of the game. There are usually challenge matches involving overseas players and occasionally the current touring side, and a county and Sunday League game to make up the programme. What can be a little disconcerting is that sometimes, during the afternoon session when the gentle click of leather on willow engenders a thoroughly soporific ambience, the peace can be rudely shattered by noises which sound like the opening exchanges of World War Three. The reason is that back at Peasholm Park, which is fairly close, miniature battleships stage naval warfare on the lake. The pyrotechnics are fantastic, and the assault on your aural senses total. As a change to cricket, it is a great spectacle.

The lake in Peasholm, which has provided great pleasure to several generations of children and their parents, is actually artificial. The collection of oriental-style bridges, waterfalls and a pagoda is augmented by a wonderful variety of exotic trees and shrubs. The park was built on what was once Northstead Manor. The stewardship of this place is held to be an 'office of profit under the crown'. Along with the better-known Chiltern Hundreds, being granted stewardship is the only way a sitting MP can leave Parliament. Holding such an office, the MP is automatically banned from sitting in the House.

To the north of Peasholm, the caravan sites begin. Before caravanning became such a popular pastime, there were large holiday camps(which were built with asbestos walls) to cater for the visitor on a budget. Along with the huge Butlin's complex at nearby Filey, these manifestations of the mid 20th century are now only a memory.

NORTH BAY c1955 S71115
An overview of North Bay taken from Castle Hill, looking north. The elegant row of houses are on Blenheim Terrace, which continues into Queens Parade. The maze of paths start as Clarence Gardens , becoming Alexandra Gardens towards in the middle distance. Although it is calm in this picture, the sea can whip around the corner in a real fury when the wind is in the wrong direction.

NORTH BAY 1891 28824
Looking south, this view of the North Bay was
taken from a slight rise at the far end of what is
now Royal Albert Drive. A water splash currently
occupies the site. The Pier has not yet succumbed
to the storms, and many bathing machines are
lined up ready for use.

NORTH BAY 1891 28825

This view is taken halfway along Royal Albert Drive. The Pier, with its theatre at the end, presented the type of pierrot shows so beloved of our Victorian forefathers. The ironwork is simple, and there are none of the stalls and side-shows often associated with this kind of structure.

THE BEACH, NORTH BAY c1955 S71071

This photograph shows none of the activity of earlier years. The motor car is starting to make its presence felt.

VIEW FROM NORTH CLIFF c1955 S71091
Here we see the north end of Royal Albert Drive. United Motor Services used to operate a bus service from here to the Spa around the Marine Drive. It was an ideal way to travel the sea front of Scarborough. On the left is the cliff railway; it survived until the 1990s, when it was dismantled and sold.

NORTH BAY 1897 39462
This picture gives an indication of the number of
people who enjoyed Clarence Gardens. Here, the
weather is clearly excellent: frilly dresses and
parasols are much in evidence. The pagoda-like
bandstand appears to be occupied: simple
entertainment by local bands were always popular.

NORTH BAY 1897 39338
This photograph shows Clarence Gardens. The entrance to the Pier can just be seen to the left of the flagpole. Gardens such as this were an essential part of Victorian life; genteel places to walk were an important component of a holiday resort. Visitors would flock here to enjoy the peace and superb floral displays.

NORTH BAY 1897 39337
Taken from a similar location, this photograph shows the angry sea. Although there is no evidence of large waves, the boiling surf stretching quite a way out to sea gives an indication of the tempests that can reign here, as they did when the Pier was swept away in 1905.

PEASHOLM PARK C1955 S71090
These ornamental pools are located higher up the valley and are fed by Peasholm Beck. The roof of a pagoda can be seen in the centre; it is situated on an island in the main lake. Note the exotic range of trees and shrubs growing here.

PEASHOLM PARK c1955 S71142
This is the main boating lake at Peasholm. Millions of visitors have enjoyed the pleasures of this lake and wandered through the grounds. The bridge in the distance leads to the island on which the pagoda is located.

PEASHOLM PARK c1955 S71140
An eternally popular part of the holidaymaker's Scarborough is the enjoyment of Peasholm Park. Boating, strolling or simply relaxing, it's all here.

HOLIDAY CHALETS C1955 S71067

Holiday chalets were an important part of the holiday scene when this view of a camp on the north bay was taken. Small buildings with Spartan facilities provided an inexpensive holiday for many people for whom even staying in a boarding house or hotel was beyond their financial reach.

HOLIDAY CHALETS AND NORTH BAY C1955 S71073

The somewhat rudimentary nature of holiday camp accommodation is clear from this picture. Since then, this area has been flattened, for demand for this type of accommodation disappeared. Touring caravan sites are now popular, and several are clustered in this northern area of town.

HOLIDAY CHALETS c1955 S71060

HOLIDAY CHALETS c1955
Entertainment in these chalet areas was essentially self-made, as this sports day illustrates. At the time, television was still a growing medium: the only channel available in Scarborough was the BBC, and only a small proportion of the population had sets. Across the road, an open air theatre provided visitor and local alike with a range of plays and shows.

HOLIDAY CHALETS c1955 S71056
Three women seem completely absorbed by the youngster's activity in the pool in the rather posed shot outside the holiday chalets. The dog in the background clearly has more interesting things to do.

HOLIDAY CHALETS c1955 S71056

The Town

ALTHOUGH there is a thriving commercial centre to Scarborough, the effect of the sea and harbour are never far away. Many of the people thronging to the fine range of elegant shops will be holidaymakers. That said, with the town the only centre of population for many miles, people from the surrounding towns and villages will also come to shop here. Several of the principal retail chains have branches in town, although the major supermarkets are generally relegated to sites on the edge of town.

The huge junction of Westborough and Northway is the location of the train station; this is an elegant building and a credit to the North Eastern Railway, who built it over a century ago. But as with most railway structures, it is now but a pale shadow of the expansive busy place that fed tens of thousands of holidaymakers into town each summer Saturday.

Across the road is a much more modern building. For years, the Odeon Cinema entertained generations of holidaymaking children and their parents, when rain spoiled their outdoor pastimes. In our own time, the entertainment has changed. In 1991, the Scarborough Theatre Development Trust took over the lease. Then in April 1996 it re-opened as The Stephen Joseph Theatre, showcasing Alan Ayckbourn's new plays.

There are several elegant bridges in the town, mainly spanning the huge ravine that is Valley Road. Nearest to the sea, the cast iron footbridge was responsible for the ease of access to the south cliffs. Further inland, the huge sweep of Valley Bridge takes the main road to Bridlington out of the town. Another iron bridge, built in 1865, was originally designed to span the Ouse at York. The county town's loss is surely Scarborough's gain.

Close to the foot of the Spa bridge is the Rotunda. This Georgian gem was designed - and still operates - as a museum. The sweeping lines of The Crescent are well worth a stroll; here is the Art Gallery, housed in a delightful Italianate building dating from 1835. Close by is Wood End, now a museum, but once the summer home of the Sitwell family.

The poet Dame Edith was born here in 1887. Originals of her work and that of brother Sir Osbert are on display here. Other buildings not to be missed are two churches. St Martin's, off the Esplanade, has several wonderful examples of Pre-Raphaelite art. St Mary's Church, on St Mary's Avenue, was built in the 12th century and extensively rebuilt three hundred years later. Being close to the Castle, it suffered severe damage when the Castle was under siege during the Civil War. Anne Bronte, who died in 1849, is buried in the churchyard here. As with many churches throughout England, St Mary's suffered under the hands of the Victorians, whose ideas of architectural excellence in churches was quite at variance with today's.

BELMONT 1890 23476

A delightful study of people taking the sea air and enjoying the view over South Bay. It provides a detailed study of both clothing and baby carriages of the period. This spot is at the end of St Nicholas Cliff, looking south over the Valley Road footbridge towards the Spa.

ST NICHOLAS CLIFF c1955 S71036

By now, cars are starting to make their presence felt, although these visitors are still blissfully unaware of a future of parking meters and pay-and-display machines. The edge of the building on the extreme left is the Grand Hotel.

VALLEY ROAD c1860 901
The exact date of this very early photograph is uncertain. The Grand Hotel is on site, possibly still under construction, for it did not open until 1867. Valley Road appears unsurfaced: dusty in summer, a quagmire in winter.

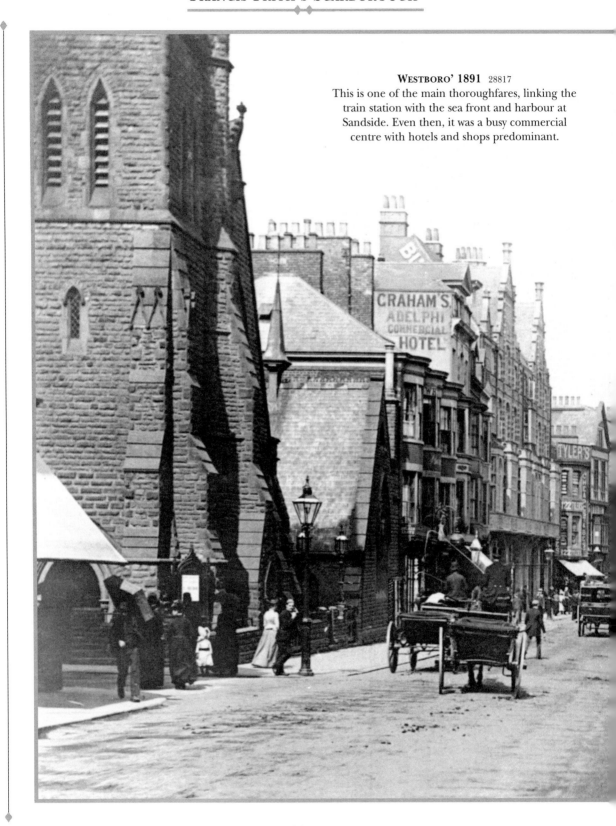

WESTBORO' 1891 28817
This is one of the main thoroughfares, linking the train station with the sea front and harbour at Sandside. Even then, it was a busy commercial centre with hotels and shops predominant.

WESTBORO' 1891 28818

Water seems the most likely cargo on the two horse-drawn carts. Several of Scarborough's main shops are grouped around this area, and the bustle of more than a century ago is reflected today.

TERRACES 1891 28819

Scarborough has long been rich in architectural splendour, as this view confirms. The exact location is not recorded, but the but the most likely candidate is The Esplanade or Queens Parade.

ST MARTINS LODGE 1891 28820
A horse and carriage stand outside St. Martins Lodge. The tower of St. Martin's church is on the left.

CHEPSTOW ROAD c1955 S710018
A couple with their young child head homeward as two girls step out searching for some fun. There is not a motor vehicle to be seen in this shot, but forty years later the street was lined on both sides by cars.

INDEX

FRITH PRODUCTS & SERVICES

Francis Frith would doubtless be pleased to know that the pioneering publishing venture he started in 1860 still continues today. More than a hundred and thirty years later, The Francis Frith Collection continues in the same innovative tradition and is now one of the foremost publishers of vintage photographs in the world. Some of the current activities include:

Interior Decoration

Today Frith's photographs can be seen framed and as giant wall murals in thousands of pubs, restaurants, hotels, banks, retail stores and other public buildings throughout the country. In every case they enhance the unique local atmosphere of the places they depict and provide reminders of gentler days in an increasingly busy and frenetic world.

Product Promotions

Frith products have been used by many major companies to promote the sales of their own products or to reinforce their own history and heritage. Brands include Hovis bread, Courage beers, Scots Porage Oats, Colman's mustard, Cadbury's foods, Mellow Birds coffee, Dunhill pipe tobacco, Guinness, and Bulmer's Cider.

Genealogy and Family History

As the interest in family history and roots grows world-wide, more and more people are turning to Frith's photographs of Great Britain for images of the towns, villages and streets where their ancestors lived; and, of course, photographs of the churches and chapels where their ancestors were christened, married and buried are an essential part of every genealogy tree and family album.

A series of easy-to-use CD Roms is planned for publication, and an increasing number of Frith photographs will be able to be viewed on specialist genealogy sites. A growing range of Frith books will be available on CD.

The Internet

Already thousands of Frith photographs can be viewed and purchased on the internet. By the end of the year 2000 some 60,000 Frith photographs will be available on the internet. The number of sites is constantly expanding, each focussing on different products and services from the Collection.

Some of the sites are listed below.

www.townpages.co.uk
www.familystorehouse.com
www.britannia.com
www.icollector.com
www.barclaysquare.co.uk
www.cornwall-online.co.uk

For background information on the Collection look at the two following sites:

www.francisfrith.com
www.francisfrith.co.uk

Frith Products

All Frith photographs are available Framed or just as Mounted Prints, and can be ordered from the address below. From time to time other products - Address Books, Calendars, Table Mats, Postcards etc - are available.

The Frith Collectors' Guild

In response to the many customers who enjoy collecting Frith photographs we have created the Frith Collectors' Guild. Members are entitled to a range of benefits, including a regular magazine, special discounts and special limited edition products.

For further information: if you would like further information on any of the above aspects of the Frith business please contact us at the address below:
The Francis Frith Collection, Frith's Barn, Teffont, Salisbury, Wiltshire England SP3 5QP.
Tel: +44 (0) 1722 716 376 Fax: +44 (0) 1722 716 881   Email: frithbook.co.uk

Frith Book Co 1999 Titles

From 2000 we aim at publishing 100 new books each year. For latest catalogue please contact Frith Book Co

Barnstaple	1-85937-084-5	£12.99	Oct 99	Maidstone	1-85937-056-X	£12.99	Sep 99
Blackpool	1-85937-049-7	£12.99	Sep 99	Northumberland & Tyne and Wear	1-85937-072-1	£14.99	Sep 99
Bognor Regis	1-85937-055-1	£12.99	Sep 99	North Yorkshire	1-85937-048-9	£14.99	Sep 99
Bristol	1-85937-050-0	£12.99	Sep 99	Nottingham	1-85937-060-8	£12.99	Sep 99
Cambridge	1-85937-092-6	£12.99	Oct 99	Oxfordshire	1-85937-076-4	£14.99	Oct 99
Cambridgeshire	1-85937-086-1	£14.99	Nov 99	Penzance	1-85937-069-1	£12.99	Sep 99
Cheshire	1-85937-045-4	£14.99	Sep 99	Reading	1-85937-087-X	£12.99	Nov 99
Chester	1-85937-090-X	£12.99	Nov 99	St Ives	1-85937-068-3	£12.99	Sep 99
Chesterfield	1-85937-071-3	£12.99	Sep 99	Salisbury	1-85937-091-8	£12.99	Nov 99
Chichester	1-85937-089-6	£12.99	Nov 99	Scarborough	1-85937-104-3	£12.99	Sep 99
Cornwall	1-85937-054-3	£14.99	Sep 99	Scottish Castles	1-85937-077-2	£14.99	Oct 99
Cotswolds	1-85937-099-3	£14.99	Nov 99	Sevenoaks and Tonbridge	1-85937-057-8	£12.99	Sep 99
				Sheffield and S Yorkshire	1-85937-070-5	£12.99	Sep 99
				Shropshire	1-85937-083-7	£14.99	Nov 99
				Southampton	1-85937-088-8	£12.99	Nov 99
				Staffordshire	1-85937-047-0	£14.99	Sep 99
				Stratford upon Avon	1-85937-098-5	£12.99	Nov 99
				Suffolk	1-85937-074-8	£14.99	Oct 99
				Surrey	1-85937-081-0	£14.99	Oct 99
				Torbay	1-85937-063-2	£12.99	Sep 99
				Wiltshire	1-85937-053-5	£14.99	Sep 99

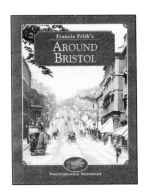

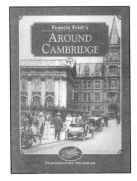

Derby	1-85937-046-2	£12.99	Sep 99
Devon	1-85937-052-7	£14.99	Sep 99
Dorset	1-85937-075-6	£14.99	Oct 99
Dorset Coast	1-85937-062-4	£14.99	Sep 99
Dublin	1-85937-058-6	£12.99	Sep 99
East Anglia	1-85937-059-4	£14.99	Sep 99
Eastbourne	1-85937-061-6	£12.99	Sep 99
English Castles	1-85937-078-0	£14.99	Oct 99
Essex	1-85937-082-9	£14.99	Nov 99
Falmouth	1-85937-066-7	£12.99	Sep 99
Hampshire	1-85937-064-0	£14.99	Sep 99
Hertfordshire	1-85937-079-9	£14.99	Nov 99
Isle of Man	1-85937-065-9	£14.99	Sep 99
Liverpool	1-85937-051-9	£12.99	Sep 99

British Life A Century Ago
246 x 189mm 144pp, hardback. Black and white Lavishly illustrated with photos from the turn of the century, and with extensive commentary. It offers a unique insight into the social history and heritage of bygone Britain.

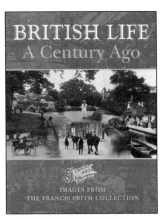

1-85937-103-5 £17.99 ....

Available from your local bookshop or from the publisher

To receive your FREE Mounted Print

Cut out this Voucher and return it with your remittance for £1.50 to cover postage and handling. Choose any photograph included in this book. Your SEPIA print will be A4 in size, and mounted in a cream mount with burgundy rule lines, overall size 14 x 11 inches.

Order additional Mounted Prints at HALF PRICE (only £7.49 each*)

If there are further pictures you would like to order, possibly as gifts for friends and family, acquire them at half price (no additional postage and handling required).

Have your Mounted Prints framed*

For an additional £14.95 per print you can have your chosen Mounted Print framed in an elegant polished wood and gilt moulding, overall size 16 x 13 inches (no additional postage and handling required).

---

* IMPORTANT!
These special prices are only available if ordered using the original voucher on this page (no copies permitted) and at the same time as your free Mounted Print, for delivery to the same address

---

Voucher
for FREE and Reduced Price Frith Prints

Picture no.	Page number	Qty	Mounted @ £7.49	Framed + £14.95	Total Cost
		1	Free of charge*	£	£
			£	£	£
			£	£	£
			£	£	£
			£	£	£
			£	£	£

	* Post & handling	£1.50
Title: AROUND SCARBOROUGH 104-3	**Total Order Cost**	£

Please do not photocopy this voucher. Only the original is valid, so please cut it out and return it to us.

I enclose a cheque / postal order for £ . . . .
made payable to 'The Francis Frith Collection'
OR please debit my Mastercard / Visa / Switch / Amex card

Number . . . .

Expires . . . . Signature . . . .

Name Mr/Mrs/Ms . . . .

Address . . . .

. . . .

. . . .

. . . .

. . . . Postcode . . . .

Daytime Tel No . . . . Valid to 31/12/01

Frith Collectors' Guild

From time to time we publish a magazine of news and stories about Frith photographs and further special offers of Frith products. If you would like 12 months FREE membership, please return this form and we will send you a New Member Pack.

Send completed forms to:
The Francis Frith Collection, Frith's Barn, Teffont, Salisbury, Wiltshire SP3 5QP

The Francis Frith Collectors' Guild

I would like to receive the New Members Pack offering 12 months FREE membership.

104-3

Name Mr/Mrs/Ms . . . .

Address . . . .

. . . .

. . . .

. . . . Postcode . . . .